ALREADY DEAD

A PLAY BY TOM AND TONY BRADMAN

Non-fiction section by Christopher Edge

PEARSON

Published by Pearson Education Limited, Edinburgh Gate, Harlow, Essex, CM20 2JE.
www.pearsonschoolsandfecolleges.co.uk

Text © Tom and Tony Bradman 2012
Non-fiction text © Christopher Edge 2012
Typeset by Kamae Design
Cover design by Wooden Ark Studio
Cover photo © radoma/Shutterstock

The rights of Tom Bradman, Tony Bradman and Christopher Edge to be identified
as authors of this work have been asserted by them in accordance with the
Copyright, Designs and Patents Act 1988.

First published 2012

15 14 13 12 11
10 9 8 7 6 5 4 3 2 1

British Library Cataloguing in Publication Data
A catalogue record for this book is available from the British Library

ISBN 9780435075330

CAUTION

Copyright notice

Printed in China (CTPS/01)

Acknowledgements

We would like to thank Biggar High School and students for their invaluable help
in the development and trialling of this book.

To Joe, with love from Uncle Tom and Grandpop.

Contents

Introduction v

Cast list viii

Prologue 1

Scene 1 5

Scene 2 13

Scene 3 23

Scene 4 33

Scene 5 43

Scene 6 53

Scene 7 65

Non-fiction:

The Dead Will Walk by Christopher Edge 77

Introduction

I like being scared. I like being terrified. I like zombies.

Zombies are, of course, not real. They're just another type of imaginary monster. They move in herds. They moan and shuffle along. They think about nothing but their next meal. They look horrible and smell even worse. They are the walking dead. Actually, that sounds a lot like the rush-hour train I used to get every day. And that's what makes them so scary. They *are* us.

Zombies are people. Originally, it was a voodoo idea. The priest would raise someone from the dead to be their unthinking slave. The living corpse would literally work until their hands fell off, and then try to carry on anyway.

But what if a zombie was sent after you? And not just any zombie. Someone you knew. One of your parents. A brother or sister. Your best friend. Could you kill them? Because however far you run, they'll keep coming. They have no mercy, no kindness, no mind. And they won't stop. Not unless you stop them.

There have been all kinds of variations of the original idea. The lumbering wreck that claws its way out of a grave and then dances in a music video. The rage-filled beast that chases you down with inhuman speed and strength. The horde of Americans that vaguely remember something from their past life and crowd around a shopping centre. The alien parasite. The magician's deceased army. The comic book superheroes brought back by a villain. But what really caught my imagination as a teenager was the idea of a zombie plague.

One zombie isn't too bad. However unpleasant it might be, however revolting it might look, I think most people could deal with a single zombie. They're weak, slow and stupid. But what about ten zombies? Fifty? A hundred? What about a whole city? Thousands, if not millions, of people. And they're not just after you. They want to eat you. Alive. Can you think of anything more terrifying than that?

It starts small. You might not know where it begins. It might be a single person. That person gets sick and then they die. Within a matter of minutes, they're awake again and hungry. The other people nearby rush over to help. Maybe they're family. Maybe they throw their arms round the sick man or woman who has miraculously recovered. That's when the zombie bites. Now there are two of them. Each one of them bites two more people. Six zombies. All six go out and each bites two more. Eighteen. And they keep going. By the time people work out what's happening, it's too late.

This is the idea that I love. The zombie epidemic. The constant threat. The idea that the whole world has turned against you. The survivors are the only reasonable, thinking creatures left. The ultimate paranormal paranoia. And that's where the power of the zombie story comes in.

Everyone has, at some time or other, felt like the only intelligent person on the planet. Everyone has wondered at how so many people can seem so stupid. Everyone has had a day when it seems like everyone is trying to drag you down. But then we've all gone along with a crowd as well. We've all done something because everyone else was doing it.

Remember, zombies aren't just monsters. They're you and me.

Sweet dreams.

Tom Bradman

Cast list

All the teenage characters are aged between fourteen and sixteen.

BOY Self-contained and tough but with secrets in his past that make him vulnerable. He wears a military jacket, combat trousers and boots, has a rucksack on his back, and carries a baseball bat stained with blood. We do not know his real name.

JAKE Over-confident and arrogant, but shaky under pressure. He likes the status of being a leader but doesn't want the responsibility when things go wrong.

LUCY Mature and confident, but not pushy. She is intelligent and sensitive – the 'mother' of the group. She carries a small medical bag.

THEO The youngest of the group and the joker. By his own admission he is a coward but he is also honest and likeable.

NAS Bullish, no-nonsense and brave to the point of recklessness. She is loyal and dependable.

ALEX	Hot-headed, but devoted to his best friend, Ben.
BEN	Quiet with a dry sense of humour.
SAM	Intelligent and self-possessed. He is in charge of communication and carries a military radio handset.
OLLIE	Nervous and the least noticed of the group. He admires Jake's confidence.
VOICES 1-8	News presenters from different stations around the UK.
ZOMBIES	The zombies do not speak but moan and groan and shuffle feet. They are dressed in rags, although we can see that once they were normal mums, dads, teachers, teenagers and even grannies. Their faces are deathly white and there are dark bloodstains round their gaping mouths and all over their chests.

Note: If this play is being performed, approximately twelve zombies would be needed to create a feeling of mass panic when they are on stage. If this play is being read aloud, then, depending on your group size, those reading Voices 1–8 could double up to provide the sound effects of the zombies in the stage directions. Alternatively, each of the main characters could also read a Voice and provide zombie sound effects.

Prologue

The stage is in darkness. Sound of radio static, sirens, shouts and terrified screaming, gunfire and moaning.

Radio static grows louder as other sounds fade, and the clear tones of news presenters cut through. The static returns as the announcements fade in and out.

VOICE 1 … the BBC news at six. The random rioting in south Wales has continued throughout the day. Nothing is known about the cause of the unrest, but there are disturbing reports of extreme violence and several deaths …   5

>   *Radio static.*

VOICE 2 … the rioting has spread into the Midlands and South West with reports of horrific scenes. Police have asked residents in the affected areas to remain in their homes, but many roads are already completely blocked …   10

>   *Radio static.*

VOICE 3 I am standing outside a school near where some of the rioters were seen earlier. Look, there's a whole mob of them! Oh my God …

they're tearing that boy apart! Watch out,
they've spotted us! Run … no, no, help, help … 15

Radio static.

VOICE 4 … we're getting reports that the rioters are
infected with some kind of disease, though
as yet no one knows how it is actually passed
on. There have been major outbreaks in East
Anglia, Yorkshire, Scotland and … 20

Radio static.

VOICE 5 … enforcing quarantine measures and a
curfew. Troops have been ordered to shoot the
infected on sight, and the Ministry of Defence
is working with the Home Office to arrange for
children still in any at-risk areas to be … 25

Radio static.

VOICE 6 … I'm sorry Professor, but I'll have to ask you
to repeat that for our listeners. I don't think I
understand what you're saying about these
people.

VOICE 7 They're dead. We're still not sure how the 30
disease spreads, but anyone infected by it dies.
It's as simple as that. The bodies then 'start'
themselves again. After that, all they want to
do is feed on living human flesh …

Radio static.

VOICE 1 … outbreaks occurring in Europe and Africa, 35
although details are unclear as we have lost

contact with several countries. Authorities are denying reports that they have fired nuclear devices in an attempt to …

Radio static.

VOICE 2 … has voted unanimously in favour of the 40 Extraordinary Powers Bill. London and other cities are to be evacuated. The royal family, prime minister and cabinet have all been flown to an unknown, safe location …

Radio static.

VOICE 6 … but professor, that's … that's insane. You 45 can't be serious!

VOICE 7 It's insane to ignore the facts. These creatures are not people. They might once have been your mother or your best friend, but now they'll rip you to pieces and eat you. You have 50 to kill them, and you have to do it fast …

Static fades, and other noises return, getting louder and louder until they stop suddenly.

Silence.

Then a single terrified voice is heard.

VOICE 8 Can anybody hear me? Please, please, is anybody there?

There is quiet sobbing, then a sound of total and utter despair.

Then silence.

Scene 1

Lights up to reveal a stage divided in two. On the left is a street of looted shops. On the right, a sports shop.

Boy sits inside the shop, talking to himself as he checks out some trainers.

BOY Well, what do you think, Sis? You're my style consultant. Is it time to ditch the boots and get back into trainers? (*listening for a second*) You say trainers would be cool, but aren't my old boots a much more sensible option for the practical   5 post-apocalyptic survivor? Fair enough …

There is shouting, screaming and moaning outside. Boy goes over to the window and looks out, raising his bat.

BOY The fools! What are they thinking? They've got no weapons! They're gonna get slaughtered …

Boy watches, shakes his head and leaves the sports shop through a concealed rear door. He takes one last backward glance before he disappears.

Jake, Lucy, Nas, Alex, Ben, Sam, Ollie and Theo enter the street from the left, all wearing face masks.

They're terrified. Everyone is running. A few stumble as they look back desperately over their shoulders.

SAM Are they still following us?

BEN I hope not. There were dozens of them! 10

ALEX More like hundreds.

THEO I didn't stop to count.

NAS You were too busy saving your skin.

THEO What else do you expect? I'm very attached to it. 15

NAS (*snorting scornfully*) Wimp.

Theo shrugs, apparently unconcerned.

SAM (*still looking behind*) They were like something out of a nightmare!

BEN Worse than any nightmare I've ever had.

NAS I reckon I could take them though, easy! 20

OLLIE With what, tough girl? Your bare hands?

NAS I'd give it a shot. Or find a weapon.

ALEX There's too many, Nas. They'd eat you alive.

LUCY But they all looked so terrible, so ill.

BEN Dead, you mean. You know they're dead? 25

LUCY Maybe they could be helped somehow.

OLLIE Yeah, right. What do we do now, Jake?

Jake moves to the front of the group and peers into the window of the sports shop that Boy had looked through.

JAKE We complete our mission. I told the captain I'd make contact with the authorities and find us some food, and that's what I'm going to do. 30

OLLIE Yeah, we should definitely stick to the plan.

LUCY Well, whatever, but I think we need to keep moving.

THEO And I think this was a bad idea. We should go back to the docks. 35

OLLIE What are you talking about? We only just got here!

BEN Theo is right, we should get back to the dinghy.

ALEX What use is that? Didn't you see the ship steaming away? They shot off as soon as they 40 saw that mob of zombies shambling towards us. Even if we make it to the dinghy, we'll never catch up with them now.

NAS It didn't look like they were coming back.

OLLIE Don't be stupid. They wouldn't abandon us, 45 would they, Jake?

JAKE No, of course not. We'll radio the captain and arrange to —

NAS Here they come again!

A group of zombies appear on the left, from where the kids entered, slowly but steadily making their way towards the group.

THEO   We're going to die, oh God, we're going to die … 5

LUCY   No we're not. Which way, Jake?

JAKE   Quick, follow me!

OLLIE   I'm with you, Jake.

> *Jake leads the group towards the back of the stage but they are soon stopped by another pack of moaning zombies, blocking their escape route.*
>
> *Jake backs off and turns to the front of the stage, but zombies appear there too.*

BEN   We're trapped!

LUCY   Come on, Jake – what now?   5

JAKE   (*beginning to panic*) I … I don't know … let me think!

LUCY   We don't have time for you to think.

NAS   We don't have time for anything.

> *The zombies press in on the kids, and one of them grabs Ollie.*

OLLIE   Get off me, you stinking zombie!   6

ALEX   They've got Ollie!

BEN   We've got to help him.

> *Ollie tries to fight the zombies off. Ben, Alex, Sam and Nas join in but the zombies drag Ollie down and swarm all over him in a feeding frenzy.*
>
> *Ben gets bitten too, and Alex pulls him away. Nas fights on for a while, but soon gives up.*

NAS There's too many! Too many!

LUCY In there, get in that shop!

> *Theo rushes into the sports shop, followed by the others.*
>
> *Alex helps the wounded Ben and stays with him.*
>
> *Lucy slams the door shut, and Sam and Nas help her block it.*
>
> *The zombies moan and bang on the door.*

SAM (*sobbing*) Did you see that? Did you see what they did to Ollie? 65

THEO They just tore him apart. (*whispering*) All that blood …

SAM The news said it was happening before we were evacuated, but I didn't believe it … 70

THEO (*beginning to get hysterical*) Well it's true! You saw it with your own eyes!

NAS (*angry, almost beside herself with rage*) We should have done something! We should have kicked some zombie butt! 75

THEO They would have killed us all!

LUCY There was nothing we could do.

ALEX Lucy, quick, over here!

> *Lucy steps towards Alex and Ben.*

JAKE Stay where you are, Lucy. I give the orders and … and we need to keep that door shut! 80

ALEX (*urgently*) Lucy, Ben is bleeding and I can't stop it!

LUCY Someone else can help here, Jake. Ben needs me.

> *Jake strides up and down in the shop, looking through the window, trying to seem in control.*

JAKE OK, right … Theo, you help Sam and Nas.

THEO (*backing away, on the verge of tears*) No way, man, 85 no way, no way …

> *Lucy goes over to Theo and puts her hands on his shoulders to calm him down. He shakes his head from side to side.*

LUCY (*gently*) Stop it, Theo. (*then more firmly*) You have to get a grip. Can you do that?

THEO (*taking a deep breath*) I … I think so …

LUCY That's good. Panicking isn't going to get 90 us anywhere.

> *Theo goes to the door and Lucy hurries over to Alex and Ben.*

> *She gets disinfectant and bandages out of her medical bag for the bite on Ben's forearm.*

> *Ben is fully conscious but cursing and groaning with pain.*

ALEX Will he be all right?

LUCY I don't see why not. It's a nasty wound, and really he should have some antibiotics, but a bite from a human doesn't usually kill you. 95

ALEX   Those things aren't human any more though,
        are they?

        Lucy doesn't speak – she just looks at Alex.

        *The zombies are getting louder, and now all of
        them are pushing at the door.*

JAKE   (*trying to stay calm*) Right, listen up everyone,
        this is what we'll do. Sam, get in touch with
        the captain, ask him where we can meet them.   100
        Then we'll work out an escape route. There
        must be a way out of here.

SAM   I'm a bit busy at the moment, Jake.

NAS   Yeah, we're only just keeping them out.

THEO   Maybe it's time for 'Plan B'.   105

NAS   What are you talking about? He doesn't have a
        'Plan B'!

JAKE   Don't worry, I'll think of something.

THEO   Soon would be good. And FYI, Lucy, I'm not
        panicking …   110

        *Just then there's a great crash at the door. There
        are screams and panic as two zombies force their
        way in.*

        *Sam and Nas manage to close the door again,
        but the zombies make for Theo, Alex, Lucy and
        Ben.*

        *Lucy stands up and blocks the zombies' path to
        Ben.*

11

THEO (*backing off, terrified*) Now I'm panicking.

> *Suddenly the concealed door opens and Boy enters the shop once more, like an avenging angel.*

> *He strides over and uses his baseball bat to take out the zombies with two sweeping blows to their heads.*

> *Everyone looks at him, amazed.*

BOY Come with me if you want to live.

JAKE Who are you? And why should I —

LUCY Let's do the introductions later. (*to Boy*) Where do we go?

BOY There's a back door. You can get out that way.

> *The group hurries towards the back door.*

> *Boy helps Sam and Nas hold the front door until the others are clear. Alex helps Ben. Lucy puts her arm round Theo's shoulders.*

> *Boy gives Sam and Nas the nod and they run. Nas grabs a baseball bat on her way out.*

> *Then Boy leaves, backing off slowly, watching as the horde of zombies shuffle across the stage, following them.*

> *Fade to black.*

Scene 2

Inside a warehouse, most of the floor bare, but with boxes stacked around the edges.

Boy leads the group onstage, alert and cautious. At last he ushers them into the warehouse and closes the door behind them.

BOY   You'll be safe in here. For the time being, anyway.

> *Alex sits Ben down against a pile of boxes to check on him. Lucy, Nas, Sam and Theo cluster round Boy. Jake, however, hangs back.*

NAS   Whoa, the way you took out those zombies was so cool, man!

SAM   We'd have been goners if you hadn't shown up.   5

LUCY   Yes, thanks, I don't know what we'd have done without you.

THEO   I'm sticking with you from now on.

BOY   (*turning to leave*) Sorry, pal. I don't carry passengers. So long.   10

The others look at each other, confused,
disappointed and scared.

SAM   Hey, you can't just walk out on us like that!

BOY   (*shrugging*) Watch me.

LUCY   But we don't even know your name.

BOY   Names don't matter anymore.

Jake pushes the others out of the way and steps
forward to confront Boy.

JAKE   Hold on a second, I'm not letting you go till I   15
       get some information. Or you can take us to
       whoever is in charge round here.

BOY   No one is in charge.

JAKE   What, no police, no army? No adults at all?

BOY   There's me, the zombies, and the dead.   20

JAKE   How did you survive, then?

BOY   Maybe the zombies think I'd taste bad.

JAKE   There must be more to it than that.

Boy shrugs and opens the door, but Lucy puts a
hand on his arm.

LUCY   Please, stay. Tell us what you know.

BOY   I don't know anything.   25

LUCY   You obviously know more than us.

JAKE   Lucy is right. (*self-importantly*) And in exchange
       I'll tell you why we're here.

BOY   I don't care why you're here.

LUCY   So why did you help us?   30

BOY   (*pausing*) It seemed like a good idea at the time.

LUCY   Well, I think it would be a good idea for us to get to know each other a little better. We survivors ought to stick together, don't you think?

BOY   No, I don't.   35

> *Boy and Lucy stare at each other intensely for a second. Then Boy sighs and nods.*

BOY   (*reluctantly*) But I'll stay. For a while.

> *Boy closes and blocks the door.*

LUCY   Great! Come on, let's settle down. I think we could all do with some quiet time after … well, after what just happened to Ollie …

> *The kids exchange glances and there is a moment of silence.*
>
> *Then Lucy, Sam, Nas and Theo pull some of the boxes into a wide semi-circle and sit on them.*
>
> *Jake takes a box in the centre. Alex and Ben remain where they are.*
>
> *Boy stands close to the door, clearly not willing to be part of the group.*

JAKE   OK, well, as I'm the leader of our mission, I'll   40
kick off —

LUCY   Hang on – we can introduce ourselves now.

JAKE   Oh, right …

> *Lucy opens her mouth, but Jake speaks first.*

JAKE   This is Lucy. She's our medic.

     Lucy gives Jake a sour look, then turns to Boy.

LUCY   Only because I did a First Aid badge at Guides.   45
     I've always wanted to be a doctor, though. I'm
     going to study medicine at uni. Or at least I
     was going to, before —

JAKE   (*talking over Lucy*) Sam is our resident tech-guy,
     the man with the radio. Sam, see if you can   50
     raise the captain, will you?

SAM   (*giving Jake a mock salute*) Aye aye, sir.

     *Sam backs away from the group slightly and talks
     quietly into his radio, only sometimes listening to
     the group's conversation and joining in.*

JAKE   This is Nas, our very own rude girl.

NAS   (*to Boy*) Can you teach me how to kill zombies?

BOY   You have to hit them in the head, always in   55
     the head.

NAS   (*nodding*) Cool, I'll bear that in mind.

JAKE   This is Theo … I don't really know why Theo
     is here.

THEO   I just wanted to get off that ship. Bored, bored,   60
     bored …

SAM   (*snorting*) Exciting enough for you so far, then?

THEO   Way too exciting. Wish I was bored now.

JAKE   As for Ollie, I don't think any of us knew him
     particularly well … (*pausing*) and over there   65

are Alex and Ben. They're best friends and they
always stick together. How's he looking, Alex?

ALEX A bit better, I think. At least the bleeding
seems to have stopped.

BEN I'm OK, although is it me or is it hot in here?   70

*Lucy goes over to check him out, and puts a hand
on his forehead.*

*Ben struggles to sit up, but can't do it and slumps
back.*

LUCY He's got a dangerously high temperature.

BOY (*under his breath, but Lucy hears him*) It always
starts like that.

JAKE Anyway, as I was saying. For the last couple
of months we've been at sea, on a ship, the   75
Constance. We were evacuated at the beginning,
just after things started getting bad, and we
soon lost touch with what was happening.

SAM Haven't had a mobile signal since the day we
went on board. In fact, we haven't had a signal   80
from anybody. No computer games on board
either …

JAKE There was enough food to keep us going for a
while, but now we're running short of supplies.
So I volunteered to lead a team into the city   85
to find some food, make contact with the
authorities, that kind of thing.

NAS (*muttering*) Trying to impress the captain again,
posh boy.

17

JAKE   Well, someone had to do something. We couldn't just stay on that ship forever, could we?

THEO   Ollie would still be alive if we had.

NAS   Ollie would still be alive if it wasn't for Jake, you mean.

JAKE   (*quietly*) That wasn't my fault.

NAS   We'll see what the captain has to say about that.

JAKE   Well, the important thing is to make sure he hasn't died for nothing. (***turning to Boy***) You still haven't told us your name.

BOY   No, I haven't.

JAKE   Why is that? Is it a secret or something?

LUCY   Leave him alone, Jake.

BOY   There's no point in telling you my name.

JAKE   What do you mean, 'no point'?

BOY   You don't need to know my name because we're not going to be friends or anything. In fact, you're probably not going to be alive for much longer. And that one over there, the one who's been bitten – he's *definitely* going to die.

ALEX   You can shut up! It's just a bite.

BOY   That's how you get the infection.

JAKE   How do you know? Before we were evacuated I heard them say they didn't know how the infection was passed on. They thought it might

be airborne. That's why I made everyone
wear masks.

BOY   I've never worn a mask and I'm not a zombie.
But I've seen plenty of people get bitten, and   120
they became zombies. All of them. You can get
infected from even the tiniest scratch, even if
the skin is only just broken.

BEN   (*faintly*) What's he saying, Alex? Am I really
going to die?   125

ALEX   Don't listen, Ben, you'll be fine, I promise!

BOY   He won't be. He'll die, just like they always do,
and then minutes later he'll turn into a zombie
and he'll come for you. Better to kill him now.
(***speaking very quietly, raising his bat***) Trust me.   130
I know.

*Everyone is horrified. Alex leaps to his feet,
furious and ready to protect his friend.*

Lucy gets between them.

*Sam doesn't notice – he's got through to the
captain.*

SAM   Quiet, everybody! I can't hear. (***into the radio
headset***) Yes, Captain, it's good to hear your
voice too. What? I'm sorry, but you're breaking
up … you'll send another dinghy to pick us   135
up at the old harbour on the other side of the
city? Great, OK … over and out! Did you hear
that, guys? They didn't abandon us!

19

JAKE See? I told you. We can keep an eye out for any supermarkets on the way, pick up some stuff at least. We can always come back for more supplies later, when we're a bit better prepared.

NAS Wait a minute. Do you even know how to get to this old harbour?

JAKE Well, no. But I'm sure we can find a map somewhere.

NAS (*to Boy*) What do *you* think, Mr Zombie killer guy?

BOY You'll be dead before you reach the end of the street. Or on your way to becoming a zombie.

THEO I bet you know how to get there, don't you?

NAS And I bet you could get us there safely, too!

Everyone is now looking at Boy hopefully.

He stares back, poker-faced.

BOY I told you, I don't carry passengers.

THEO Great, so you'll just leave us to die. What if we follow you anyway?

BOY You couldn't keep up.

NAS I could. You and me, we'd make a great team.

JAKE Forget it, everyone. We don't need him.

LUCY Of course we do.

Lucy puts her hand on Boy's arm and looks into his eyes as intensely as before.

LUCY   Maybe he needs us too. 160

BOY   (*very softly, holding her gaze*) I don't need anybody.

LUCY   (*to Boy*) But you'll help us, won't you?

> *There is a moment of silence, and Boy sighs and nods.*

> *Everybody relaxes.*

BOY   But you all have to do what I say, as soon as I say it. (*pointing at Ben*) And if you won't finish him off, we leave him behind. 165

ALEX   What are you talking about? I'm not doing that!

BEN   (*almost crying*) Don't leave me, Alex, not with those things outside.

> *Alex lunges at Boy. The others hold him back.*

JAKE   Relax, Alex. It's my call. Of course we'll take Ben with us. 170

> *Alex gives Boy one last glare, then returns to Ben.*

BOY   (*shaking his head*) Suit yourselves. But don't come crying to me when he turns.

> *Fade to black.*

Scene 3

A street with a bus shelter to one side.

The kids walk in a line, led by Boy. Nas is at the rear swinging her bat and trying to impress Boy. Theo follows Boy very closely. Alex helps Ben along. No one is wearing a mask any more.

Suddenly Ben starts coughing.

BEN It's no good, Alex. I'll have to sit down for a while.

ALEX (*to Boy*) Can we stop here? Ben needs to rest.

THEO I could do with a rest too. And a drink.

BOY (*sighing*) Three minutes, that's all.

> *Boy pulls a military water bottle out of his rucksack and hands it to Theo, who nods his thanks and glugs away, then passes it to Sam and Nas.*

ALEX (*to Boy*) You know, I really don't like you. 5

BOY (*shrugging*) OK, make it two minutes.

ALEX You evil son of a —

LUCY Enough, Alex. I'll help you get Ben into this shelter.

23

Lucy and Alex take Ben into the shelter and lay him down. Lucy looks at the bite and frowns as she checks his temperature again.

Theo is nervous. Sam keeps checking his radio. Boy nods to Nas and gets her to keep an eye out to the left, while he watches the right.

Jake hovers uselessly behind Lucy, trying to look in charge.

LUCY How are you feeling, Ben?

BEN (*coughing*) Oh, peachy, just absolutely fine. But the really big question on my mind is … will I ever play the piano again?

ALEX Don't listen to him, Lucy. Him and I have been friends since primary school. He gave up the piano after two lessons.

BEN Not true. After the first lesson. It was all too difficult – white keys, black keys, pedals …

Ben coughs even more, and retches.

THEO He doesn't look too good. In fact he looks a bit like … a zombie.

ALEX (*yelling angrily*) Shut up, you moron! That's a terrible thing to say!

BOY (*quietly angry*) Hey! Keep your voice down. It's noise that brings them.

JAKE What do you mean? I thought you didn't know anything.

BOY   The zombies are attracted by noise. Breaking glass, loud voices, engine sounds. Did your dinghy have an engine?

The others glance at each other.

BOY   And yelling, definitely yelling. If they hear you, they'll come.   30

JAKE   (*aggressively*) But you said there weren't any near here.

BOY   No, I said I hadn't *seen* any in the streets round here for a while. All these buildings could be   35
full of them.

THEO   (*moving closer to Boy*) Really? Shouldn't we get going, then?

SAM   (*uneasily*) Yeah, I'm with you on that, Theo.

NAS   (*muttering*) Obviously being a wimp is   40
infectious too.

ALEX   (*angry, frustrated*) But Ben can't go on. He's weak and burning up.

JAKE   We should take him to the nearest hospital. Maybe you could find some medicine that   45
would help him, Lucy. And you never know, some proper doctors might even still be hiding there.

LUCY   (*frowning*) Thanks for the vote of confidence, Jake.   50

ALEX   But it's a great idea, Lucy! Every city has a hospital.

LUCY (*sighing*) I suppose it's worth a try. I can't really do much for him with what I've got in my bag.

Lucy turns to look questioningly at Boy, but he just shakes his head.

BOY The hospital is the worst place we could go.

ALEX (*furious*) Oh yeah? And why is that?

BOY Where do you think everybody was taken when they got sick, at least to begin with? The hospital is one huge zombie nest. The only doctors you'll find there will be zombies themselves.

SAM Damn, the guy really does know how to make you feel bad.

NAS He tells it the way it is. That's cool with me.

Suddenly Ben starts to retch and cough even more than before. He moans, too, and starts thrashing.

Alex tries to hold on to him, but Ben throws him off.

ALEX Oh my God, Ben! Please, Lucy, help him!

LUCY (*backing away now, almost crying*) I can't, I can't …

BOY (*stone-faced*) Nobody can.

Ben's arms and legs are flailing. He moans and wails loudly, and then dies at last with a final shudder.

The others are shocked and silent. Alex is distraught and hugs Ben, crying.

26

ALEX (*to Boy, yelling loudly*) Happy now? Happy you were right? Happy that my best friend is dead?

BOY He won't be dead long. We have to put him out of action then get moving. The zombies **70** are bound to have heard all the noise.

Boy steps forward, his bat raised, and Alex stands to meet him.

Jake and Sam step forward next to Alex but Lucy and Nas move towards Boy.

Theo freezes.

SAM You can't do that to his friend!

JAKE No you can't, I won't let you.

ALEX I don't believe he's right anyway.

NAS Don't be stupid, he knows about this stuff! **75**

THEO (*panicking, almost hysterical*) Come on, let's go, let's go!

ALEX (*to Boy*) You'll have to kill me first.

BOY (*quietly*) No problem.

ALEX (*squaring up*) OK then, take your best shot … **80**

Suddenly, unnoticed by the group, one of Ben's fingers twitches … then another, then one of his feet starts to move.

LUCY Calm down, you two. This is all getting out of hand. Alex, you're just upset about Ben – we all are.

JAKE   Your new boyfriend doesn't look all that upset
to me, Lucy. In fact he looks as if he's having
the time of his life.

LUCY   (*sighing*) He's not my boyfriend, Jake.

JAKE   I'm glad to hear it. How do we know if
anything he says is true? He might just be
some nutjob who's latched on to us.

SAM   Steady on, Jake. That's going a bit far.

NAS   And he did happen to save our lives, posh boy.

JAKE   It might have looked that way to you, Nas. But
I had the situation well under control. I would
have got us out of there even if he hadn't
appeared.

THEO   Under control? We'd all be dead now if it was
up to you!

LUCY   Listen, can we all stop arguing? It's not
helping, is it?

JAKE   (*giving Theo a hard stare*) You're right, Lucy.
(*nodding in Boy's direction*) And he's the reason
we're arguing. So I'm making an executive
decision. (*to Boy*) We don't need you any more,
whatever your name is. I'm the leader, and I'll
decide what we do.

BOY   (*shrugging*) That's fine with me.

Boy turns to go, but Lucy grabs his arm.

*A sudden low moan makes them all stop what
they're doing and turn round to look at Ben.*

The moaning is coming from him, and he sits up like a jack-in-the-box. He looks exactly like a zombie now, and is soon on his feet.

Alex moves towards him.

ALEX (*delighted*) Ben? Are you all right, mate? That's quite some recovery!

Alex turns round to grin at the others, who have stepped back, their instincts telling them there is something very wrong with Ben.

Boy stands his ground raising his bat ready to strike.

Suddenly Ben lurches forward, grabbing for Alex.

SAM (*yelling*) Watch out, Alex! 110

Ben grabs hold of Alex and tries to bite his arm.

Alex begins to realise his friend is now a zombie, and attempts to push him off. They struggle.

Sam, Nas, Theo, Lucy and Jake are frozen in horror.

Boy steps forward, grabs Ben and throws him to one side. He raises his bat ready to strike Ben.

Suddenly a low moaning can be heard and a crowd of zombies shuffles onstage from the left.

BOY (*angrily*) You see? I told you! Every zombie in the city is probably heading our way right now! I should let them kill the lot of you.

LUCY You're not going to though, are you?

BOY (*looking at her, then sighing, defeated*) All of you,   1
get behind me!

NAS (*stepping up beside Boy*) I can fight too!

BOY We'll head for the end of the street.

SAM Look out, here they come!

The first few zombies are on top of them.

Boy takes out one, then two more.

*Nas wildly swings her bat, then finally connects
properly with a zombie's head.*

THEO (*clearly impressed*) Go, Nas! I feel safer already.   1

NAS (*finishing off another zombie*) You'd feel even
safer if you helped.

THEO I can't, it's against my beliefs.

NAS What are you talking about?

THEO I'm a practising coward.   1.

*More zombies arrive, but Boy and Nas hold them
off, covering the retreat.*

*Then suddenly Alex runs towards the zombies. He
has caught sight of Ben, who has joined the other
zombies in the attack.*

SAM Alex! What are you doing? Don't be a fool.

*Alex tries to grab Ben, but the zombies grab Alex
and pull him down to devour him in a feeding
frenzy.*

The group huddles together on the far side of the stage, unable to look.

BOY That will keep them busy. Follow me.

LUCY Where are you taking us?

BOY To the safest place I know.

THEO Thank God, thank God.   130

BOY (*coldly*) Not that you lot deserve it. And I only hope we make it there before nightfall. We'll be zombie food if we don't.

THEO Why did you have to go and spoil it? Hey, wait for me!   135

The kids exit stage right, with Boy leading and Theo scurrying along at the tail.

One or two of the zombies look up, but most just keep on feeding.

Ben shoves the other zombies out of the way and dives in with a howl.

Blackout.

Scene 4

A dim red bulb glows on the left side of the stage.

A door opens beneath the bulb and the group stumble onstage – Theo first, followed by Sam, Jake, Lucy, then Nas, who backs in with her bat raised. They're all out of breath and wide-eyed.

Boy comes in last. He quietly shuts the steel door and lowers a thick metal bar across it.

THEO (*breathing a sigh of relief*) Now that's the kind of door I like.

BOY (*snapping*) Stay where you are and don't touch anything.

> *Boy crosses the stage into the shadow, the others stand very still.*
>
> *Lights up to reveal Boy's hideout. It was once a sizeable office, but the desk has been pushed to one side and a camp bed stands in its place.*
>
> *There are several plastic boxes containing military clothes. There's a camping stove in a corner, with pots and pans and tins of food stacked beside it.*

33

There's also an armchair facing a TV, a laptop and a games console on a box and a full bookcase.

A window stretches along the entire wall above the desk.

NAS (*to Boy, nodding thankfully*) This is your place, is it? Cool.

Boy doesn't reply.

SAM I don't believe it … hey guys, check out what's down there.

Sam is standing by the window, and Jake, Nas and Theo go over to join him. They look down in wonder. Boy and Lucy stay where they are, looking at each other.

NAS Whoa, it's a warehouse full of stuff!

SAM Looks like mostly tinned food.

THEO But are those freezer cabinets too?

JAKE (*to Boy*) I'm impressed. You really have set yourself up very nicely. It's good of you to bring us here.

BOY (*angrily*) No, it's not. I had no choice. You lot are a disaster, a walking disaster. If we'd stayed out there any longer you'd have been dead, and me too.

SAM Hey, thanks for the sympathy, man. I mean, I'm sure we're all very grateful for the help you've given us, but in case you hadn't noticed, we've just lost another two of our friends.

BOY I told you what to do, but you didn't listen. If you'd finished off the one who'd been bitten, the other one would still be alive.   25

JAKE What, so it's our fault Alex is dead?

NAS Not *our* fault. Just yours, posh boy. You were the one who said we should bring Ben with us.

JAKE It was the zombies who killed Alex, not me!

THEO He's got a point there, Nas.   30

Nas glares at Theo.

THEO I'm only saying.

NAS No one is going to listen to you again, Jake. You just keep your mouth shut. (*rising to confront him*) Let me make this perfectly clear. You are *not* our leader.   35

Jake looks at the others. Nas, Theo and Sam just stare at him, but Lucy shakes her head.

JAKE (*angry now, but keeping himself under control*) Fine. Do what you like. See if I care.

NAS Don't worry, we will.

LUCY Look, this isn't getting us anywhere. What's done is done. We have to decide what to do from now on.   40

SAM (*nodding at Boy*) Doesn't that depend on him? It sounds to me as if he's had enough of us. Maybe he wants us to leave.

THEO (*shaking his head*) He'll have to make me.

NAS (*snorting*) That wouldn't be so hard. Especially not for him.

SAM But we can't leave now. It's dark out there.

LUCY (*quietly, to Boy*) I don't think you want us to leave. You know we couldn't make it without you.

There is a moment of silence as Lucy holds Boy's gaze. At last Boy looks away from her and sighs.

BOY OK, here's the only deal I'm prepared to offer. You can stay tonight, and I'll take you to the old harbour tomorrow. But when we're outside you have to do what I say, when I say it. If you don't I'll just leave you for the zombies. You'll look round and I'll be gone. Is that clear?

SAM OK by me.

THEO Absolutely.

NAS No problem.

JAKE I'm not sure, I mean —

NAS I told you to keep your mouth shut, posh boy.

Nas stares at Jake until he looks away furiously.

NAS Right. We're all yours, Mr Zombie Killer.

Boy looks at them and shakes his head once more in disbelief. He drops his rucksack on the floor and props his bat against the wall so it's within reach of the bed.

SAM Well, now that's settled, is there any chance of getting something to eat? I don't know about anyone else, but I'm starving.

BOY (*sighing again*) You don't want much, do you?   65
I'll make something …

LUCY No, we should cook for you. It's the least we
can do. We'll need more than you've got in
here, though.

BOY Fair enough. (*nodding towards the corner*) The   70
stairs down to the warehouse are over there.

LUCY I don't suppose you've got any more medical
supplies, have you?

BOY (*giving her the briefest of smiles*) Furthest aisle,
far end. I stored some camping gear near there   75
too. You might find a few sleeping bags.

LUCY Great! Nas, Sam, Theo, you're with me.

*The four of them head for the warehouse, leaving
Boy and Jake alone.*

*Jake looks down into the warehouse, deep in
thought. He nods to himself at last, takes a deep
breath, lets it out. Then he turns to Boy.*

JAKE I'm sorry about what happened earlier
between you and me. I think we might have
got off to a bad start out there.   80

BOY You could say that.

JAKE Well, can we put it all behind us? I have to say I
think you've done an amazing job of surviving.
It can't have been easy.

BOY You could *definitely* say that.   85

JAKE I've got so many questions to ask you.

BOY Make it a few.

JAKE OK then … how come you ended up living in this place?

BOY It made sense. Why go looking for food all over the place when there was probably lots of it under one roof? This was a distribution depot for one of the big supermarket chains. It didn't take me long to find it.

JAKE You've got electricity, though. How did you manage that?

BOY There's a generator in case of power cuts, with enough diesel to last quite a while. It's in the basement, so the zombies can't hear it.

JAKE But how did you make the whole place safe? It's so big … and didn't the people who worked here get turned into zombies too?

BOY It was empty when I found it, and all the doors were open. But once I got them closed and made sure the alarms were turned off it was OK.

JAKE Tell me more about the zombies. Why haven't they all starved? You said yourself there are no normal people left for them to eat.

BOY I haven't seen any animals in the city for a while. Maybe the zombies are eating cats and dogs. Or rats. They'd much rather eat something like you, though. More meat on the bone.

JAKE (*thinking for a second*) You're pretty good with that bat. But surely you'd be able to kill them more easily with a gun?

BOY Too noisy. When the army came they just drew more and more zombies towards them until they were overwhelmed. Better to be quiet and get away from them. The zombies don't move very quickly. **120**

JAKE I see, that's all really useful information, thanks. (*pausing*) Oh, one last thing. I was wondering if you could tell me something about the route we'll be taking to the old harbour in the morning. I mean, just in case we get separated. **125**

There's another moment of silence. Boy stares hard at Jake, then he picks up his rucksack, takes out a map and goes to the desk to unfold it. Jake follows and looks over his shoulder.

BOY This is where we are, and this is the old harbour. This is the best route to take – up this road, across the park, then along the coast road. We need to stay away from the areas I've marked in red – big zombie nests. **130**

Jake listens intently, his eyes on the map.

Just then the others return, loaded down with boxes of food and sleeping bags. Lucy has a couple of carrier bags full of medical supplies.

Boy re-folds the map but leaves it on the desk.

THEO Things are looking up. We've got burgers!

SAM (*laughing*) Sausages and crisps, too.

JAKE Well thanks a lot, guys. There isn't much for me there. I'd better go down and see if there's anything for a vegetarian to eat.

NAS You're a vegetarian? That explains a lot.

THEO Good job you haven't been infected, then. You'd make a lousy zombie.

> *Theo, Sam and Nas laugh, then work on getting the meal ready. Jake ignores them and heads down to the warehouse. Lucy sits beside Boy on his bed.*

LUCY I don't know how we can ever thank you properly. I was running out of supplies but now I've got plenty of bandages and plasters, lots of disinfectant, a couple of boxes of painkillers, even some antibiotics —

BOY (*shrugging, cutting her off*) No problem.

LUCY (*pausing*) You're coming with us, aren't you? On the ship, I mean.

BOY (*glancing at her*) I don't think so.

LUCY But you can't stay here alone. You don't have to any more.

BOY Maybe I like being on my own.

LUCY I don't believe that.

BOY Believe what you like.

LUCY (*quietly*) I was on my own for a while. Then I was picked up by the army and taken to the ship. It seemed like one minute the world was normal, and the next it all fell to pieces. My parents were on holiday and my brother was away at uni. I don't know what happened to them.

BOY You'd better hope they're dead.

LUCY Why do you say that? 160

BOY (*shrugging*) It's easier that way. For them. And for you.

LUCY (*looking at Boy intently*) What happened to you? What made you this way?

Boy looks away and doesn't answer.

NAS (*interrupting*) Come on, you two. Stop 165 smooching – dinner is ready!

THEO Hey, hang on a second – we don't have any plates!

SAM Who needs them? We're post-apocalyptic survivors! 170

THEO You can do what you want, but I'm not letting my standards drop.

There is general jeering and laughter, and the food is handed out. Nas, Theo and Sam settle down in a circle near the bed, and Boy and Lucy start eating too.

Nobody takes any notice of Jake when he returns with a couple of cans of vegetables. He slips the folded map into his pocket as he passes the desk.

Fade to black.

Scene 5

A dim red bulb is glowing on the left side of the stage, revealing the shapes of bodies wrapped up in sleeping bags.

Sam is asleep in the armchair, cradling an Xbox controller. Theo is in the camp bed; the others on the floor.

Suddenly an industrial alarm goes off. Boy is instantly on his feet, bat in hand; the others are slower to wake.

THEO (*sleepily*) What … what's going on? I was having a lovely dream. I was at home, tucked up safe and sound in my bed, and none of this had happened.

NAS (*irritated*) I still can't believe he let you sleep in   5
the bed and I had to sleep on the floor. It's not fair. And can somebody turn that alarm off? It's seriously doing my head in.

LUCY (*slightly anxious*) Where is it coming from?

NAS (*putting her hands over her ears*) Everywhere.   10

43

SAM I was dreaming too. I thought the alarm was part of a game. Boy, did I have fun playing on the Xbox last night. Never thought I'd see one again. I'll die happy now. Wait … what am I saying? (*suddenly uneasy*) Hang on … isn't that noise going to attract the zombies?

NAS (*shrugging*) So what if it does? We should be safe enough in here.

> *Boy looks down through the window into the warehouse and frowns, deeply puzzled.*

> *He turns round, scans the room and sees that Jake is missing. His face drops.*

BOY (*furious*) I wouldn't be so sure about that. Not after what your friend has done.

LUCY (*sitting up and looking round the room as well*) You mean Jake? Where is he? What do you mean? What has he done?

> *The familiar moaning and shuffling of feet can be heard.*

> *Boy looks down into the warehouse again and frowns even more. The zombies are already inside.*

THEO (*slowly standing up, scared*) They're coming, I can hear them!

LUCY Calm down, Theo. I'm still trying to work out what's happening. (*to Boy*) Please, tell me what you think Jake has done.

BOY (*coldly*) Your friend has turned the alarms back on. All he had to do then was hit one of the emergency buttons to set them off. He's opened the warehouse doors, too. Every single one of them. 30

LUCY (*getting out of her sleeping bag*) But that's crazy! Why would he do such a thing? 35

SAM (*standing up too, putting the Xbox controller down behind him on the chair*) Oh … my … God. He's screwed us. Jake has totally screwed us.

NAS (*scrambling out of her sleeping bag*) Whoa, back up there a little, Sam. This is all way too complicated for me, especially in the middle of the night. I know Jake is a creep, but just how has he screwed us? 40

SAM Think about it, Nas! Jake wants to be a hero, so he's decided he's going to be the first one to tell the captain about this place. Then he can lead another team back to collect the food. They'll probably give him a medal! 45

LUCY (*shaking her head*) But I still don't understand why he opened all the doors and set the alarms off. What does that achieve? 50

BOY He doesn't just want to be the first one. He wants to be the *only* one.

Sam exchanges a look with Boy and nods. There's a pause as the others take in what Boy has said.

The alarms are still whooping and the sounds of moaning and shuffling feet are getting louder.

THEO (*shocked*) You mean he wants the zombies to get us.

LUCY I don't believe it. I don't believe he would do   5
that …

NAS I do. He doesn't care about us. He only cares about himself.

SAM It makes a lot of sense from his point of view.
He doesn't want us around to spoil his story by   6
telling the captain how useless he's been. It's not
his food anyway, so it would probably be best to
get rid of the owner, too. And the zombies won't
hang around long after they've eaten all of us.

NAS He's not going to make it though, is he? He   6
doesn't know how to get to this old harbour
place.

BOY (*shaking his head*) He got me to show him the
route on a map. (*nodding at the desk*) I left the
map there, but it's gone.   7

LUCY Can't we just radio the captain and tell him the
truth?

SAM Hey, great idea – why didn't I think of it?
(*looking for his radio*) Where's my radio? I'm
certain I put it down beside the chair when I   7
was playing on the Xbox.

His efforts to find the radio become more and more desperate.

46

*Nas, Theo and Lucy join in the search as well, but
they eventually give up.*

NAS Jake's taken it, hasn't he? Why, that evil,
double-crossing … I'm going to kill him. I'm
going to track him down and I'm going to beat
his head in.   80

THEO We've got to get out of here first. That's what
we're going to do, right?

LUCY But why do we have to leave? The zombies
can't get up here, can they?

BOY (*quietly, a strange smile on his face*) Yes, they can.   85
The door at the top of the stairs won't hold
them for long. They'll soon break it down.

SAM And if we don't get to the dinghy before Jake
the ship will leave without us. I don't know
about you lot, but I'd rather be on it.   90

NAS So what's the problem? We just leave by the
other door.

*Suddenly there's another noise, a dull booming.
Zombie fists are pounding on the steel door
and Nas, Theo, Sam and Lucy turn to look at it,
horrified.*

THEO Don't tell me. It's too late to go out the way we
came in.

SAM OK then, what do we do now?   95

NAS (*picking up her baseball bat*) I say we go down into
the warehouse and crack some zombie skulls.

Then we can close the doors, turn off the alarms, stay quiet and wait for the rest to go away.

Boy moves to the centre of the stage. He stands very still, his eyes tightly closed and fists clenched, seemingly unaware of what is happening around him. Lucy doesn't move either – she stands and watches Boy.

SAM (*looking down into the warehouse*) That's not going to work. There are too many of them inside already.

THEO Why don't we just block the door to the warehouse and stay quiet?

SAM They're still going to keep coming all the time they can hear the alarm, and that could keep going for weeks, depending on the generator. We'd probably end up starving to death.

THEO I don't like that idea much. It would be even worse knowing all that lovely food was sitting down there.

NAS And I don't want to sit around just waiting to die anyway. I say we open the main door and go for them, fight our way through.

SAM But what if there are hundreds out there already? We'll never make it. If you ask me we've had it, this is game over.

THEO Tell me you don't think he's right, Nas, please!

NAS Hold on … I don't know why I'm even talking
to you two! The zombie killer is the man with
the answers. He'll know what to do.

*They all stop talking. Theo, Nas, Sam and Lucy
circle Boy and stare.*

*He doesn't respond at first, but then he opens his
eyes and looks round at them, his face stony.*

BOY Stupid, stupid, stupid.

SAM Hey, who are you calling stupid?

*Boy laughs and Sam, Nas and Theo look at him
in surprise.*

BOY Me. I'm the stupid one. Should have known,
should have known …

*Sam, Nas and Theo all look at each other,
nervous and bewildered.*

NAS Listen, no one's blaming you for what's
happened. You couldn't have known Jake
would be such a —

Boy's laughter stops as if it's been turned off.

BOY I'm not talking about that. I should have known
it would come to this again, my having to save
people who can't save themselves. People who
go out of their way to get themselves killed
however hard you try to help them.

Lucy goes over to him, puts her hand on his arm.

LUCY (*quietly*) Is that what happened?

49

BOY (*shaking off her hand*) I don't want to talk about it.

Suddenly there's a loud crash from the direction of the door to the warehouse. Theo, Nas and Sam look that way, startled.

THEO So is that it? We're not going to do anything? You had a bad time with some useless people in the past and because of that we have to die?

SAM That sucks.

NAS Come on, Killer, don't let us down. I know you can do it, I know you can save us.

LUCY I bet she's right. I can't believe you don't have an escape route.

Boy looks at her and at the others once more. He's clearly struggling with his feelings. He takes a deep breath and shakes his head as if he knows he has no choice.

BOY Help me move the desk.

NAS (*grinning*) Now you're talking.

Boy takes one end of the desk with Sam while Theo and Nas take the other. They shift it in Boy's direction, and a trap door is revealed.

BOY (*pulling up the door*) This gives access to the under-floor cables. I thought I might need another way out when I moved in, so I broke through the floor into the office below. From there we can get to the basement.

SAM But what if we get trapped down there?

BOY We won't. There's an entrance to the sewers.

THEO Great. We're going to be up to our necks in —

NAS It's either that or end up as zombie food.
Very soon. **155**

> *The crashing at the door to the stairs from
> the warehouse intensifies, as does the zombie
> moaning and the pounding on the main door.*

BOY OK. Time to leave. (*to Nas*) You first.

NAS (*grabbing her baseball bat*) You're the boss.

THEO I'll be right behind you.

NAS Why am I not surprised?

> *They disappear through the trap door, and Boy
> gives Lucy the nod to go next. Boy nods at Sam
> to follow, but Sam pauses and heads back to the
> armchair.*

BOY What are you doing? We don't have time! **160**

SAM (*grabbing the Xbox*) I'm not leaving this little
beauty behind —

> *Just then there's an even louder crash and the
> sound of breaking glass.*
>
> *The zombies have finally broken through the
> door at the top of the stairs, and several shuffle
> in, cutting Sam off from the trap door.*
>
> *Boy takes one out with his bat, but Sam is pulled
> down screaming by the rest. Boy looks away, slips
> into the trap door and shuts it firmly behind him.*
>
> *Fade to black.*

Scene 6

The sewers.

A beam of light can be seen, then Nas comes onstage holding a torch, followed by Theo, then Lucy, who also has a torch, and finally Boy.

They're crouched and moving slowly, wading through the water. Nas and Theo are struggling with the smell. Lucy keeps checking for Boy, who is lagging some way behind.

Eventually he stops and sits in an alcove, head in hands, his face covered.

LUCY Nas, Theo, hang on a second …

Nas and Theo stop and come back. They stand awkwardly, looking at Boy.

NAS (*concerned, to Lucy*) Is he OK? He hasn't said a word since he told us about Sam. I know he doesn't usually say much, but even so …

THEO (*nervously*) He better be OK. We're all counting on him. 5

LUCY (*sternly*) I think it would be better if you kept that kind of remark to yourself, Theo. That's just the kind of pressure he could probably do without.

THEO Sorry I spoke, I'm sure.

NAS Come on, Theo. Let's check out where this sewer leads.

THEO No thanks. I think we ought to stick together.

Nas pulls Theo by the arm and glares at him.

NAS That wasn't a suggestion. It was an order. (*whispering*) They need to talk.

THEO What? Oh, I get it. Fair enough, I suppose. But we're not going far, are we? It's pretty dark and scary up ahead, even with a torch.

NAS For heaven's sake, Theo, stop wittering!

Nas drags Theo off into the shadows.

The torch beam disappears offstage, leaving Boy and Lucy alone.

LUCY (*watching them go*) I'm sorry. You probably didn't want to hear that.

BOY (*shrugging*) He was only telling the truth. You *are* counting on me.

LUCY And you don't want us to.

BOY You're right, I don't.

LUCY But we don't have any choice. We'd all be dead if not for you.

BOY (*looking up at her*) Actually, for some reason I'm the one who doesn't seem to have any choice. [30] I keep trying to get away from you but you won't let me. And if you hadn't noticed, most of your friends *are* dead now.

LUCY (*impatiently*) You know, I just don't get it. What is your problem? Why are you being so [35] horrible? I'm beginning to think you hate us.

BOY Maybe I do. You're people. People are my problem.

LUCY Not the zombies, then?

BOY (*laughing*) No, not the zombies. They're dead [40] simple. They'll eat you if they can. And if you smack them in the head, they leave you alone.

LUCY It almost sounds as if you admire them.

BOY I don't. But they're a lot easier to get along with. People are much more difficult. Much [45] more complicated.

LUCY This is all to do with whatever happened to you, isn't it?

BOY You don't give up, do you? You're like a dog with a bone. You remind me of somebody. [50] In more ways than one.

LUCY Who? A girlfriend?

BOY (*pausing*) My sister.

LUCY Tell me about her.

BOY Do I have to? [55]

LUCY I think you probably do.

> *Boy looks at her for a second, then shakes his head and gives one last enormous sigh.*
>
> *Boy then leans back, folds his arms and closes his eyes.*

BOY (*softly*) She was the one who held it together, at least to begin with. She kept Mum and Dad going, said we had to help as many of our friends and neighbours as we could. But they all did stupid things and I soon realised how dangerous that was.

LUCY Stupid things? Like what?

BOY (*opening his eyes*) The kind of things your friends did. Telling themselves that someone who had been bitten was going to be OK. Going back into a house full of zombies to get a stupid computer game.

LUCY What else did you expect? That's the way people are.

BOY And that's exactly why most people got eaten or turned into zombies. I could see the way things were going and I tried to tell her we ought to forget everyone else and just look after ourselves. But she wouldn't listen.

LUCY (*smiling*) You're right, she does sound like me.

BOY So I decided I'd just have to take care of her and Mum and Dad, be their protector. But it was too difficult, much too difficult … the zombies got them in the end. Then I was on my own, like you.

LUCY No, not like me. I always wanted to be with people.

BOY Can you blame me? Most people are their own worst enemies. You have to be ruthless if you want to survive. Single minded, ready to do whatever it takes. Kill anyone who gets bitten, even if it's your … your …

Boy turns away.

LUCY That must have been really hard.

BOY (*turning to look at her*) And then you lot turn up and I get drawn in. After I swore I'd never have anything to do with people again. That I'd never let anyone depend on me again.

LUCY That you'd never let yourself fail again.

BOY Maybe. That's up to me though, isn't it?

LUCY Of course it is. But I don't believe you really feel that way. Sure, people can do stupid things, but sometimes they don't, and it's helping each other that makes us human. The people you love, your friends – they make life worth living. Without them you're *already* dead. You might as well be a zombie.

Pause.

BOY Easy enough for you to say.

LUCY   It's true, though. And getting you to stay with
us wasn't that hard. You could have walked   10
away at any time. You could walk away now,
leave me and Nas and Theo in this sewer and
we'd never be able to find you.

BOY   (*frowning*) Don't think I haven't thought about it.

LUCY   I'm sure you have. But you're like most boys.   11
All talk.

They stop speaking and look at each other.

BOY   (*half-smiling*) That's just the kind of thing she
would have said.

LUCY   I wish I'd known her. She sounds cool. I know
what else she would probably have said too.   11

BOY   Oh yeah? I have a feeling you're going to tell me.

LUCY   Let me ask you a question first.

BOY   What is it with you lot and questions?

Lucy gives him a puzzled look.

BOY   Never mind. Fire away.

LUCY   OK, then – how do you see things working out   12
for you in the future?

BOY   (*puzzled*) I don't think about it. I take one day at
a time.

LUCY   Well, let me tell you what I think will happen
to you if you carry on this way. You'll probably   1
find somewhere else to hole up. Somewhere
you can make just as secure and that has
another generator and plenty of food.

BOY I might already have somewhere in mind.

LUCY But all the diesel will run out eventually, and   130
you can't live on tinned food forever. Have you
heard of botulism?

Boy shakes his head.

LUCY It's a disease you can get from old tinned food.
A disease that can kill you. Or you might starve
to death, or get ill in the winter and die, or cut   135
yourself on something and die hideously of
gangrene. You might even get caught by the
zombies.

BOY (*shrugging*) We all have to die one way or the
other.   140

LUCY But you don't have to die alone. Is that what
you think your sister and your mum and dad
would have wanted? They wouldn't want you
to live like this either. Although it's not living, is
it? It's just … just *existing*.   145

Pause.

Boy looks intently at Lucy.

BOY So what are you offering me instead?

LUCY Life. Real life, with messy, chaotic people who
do stupid things. People who will argue about
what to do and how to do it. But who will also
worry about you and care for you and maybe   150
even make you laugh sometimes.

BOY But what if you all end up counting on me? I'm
not sure I can handle that.

LUCY Why? You're good at surviving, at being a
      leader and taking care of people. I bet you
      kept your sister and your parents alive longer
      than anyone else could have done. And you
      said yourself you could have saved more of us
      if we'd listened to you. Maybe we will in future.
      What was your sister's name?

      Pause.

BOY   (*very quietly*) Abby. Her name was Abby.

LUCY Well, Abby would have told you to jump at
      this chance.

      Pause.

      Then Boy smiles a proper smile at Lucy.

BOY   You'd be wasted as a doctor.

LUCY What do you mean?

BOY   You'd make a great careers advisor.

LUCY (*laughing*) So can I take that as a yes? (*holding out
      a hand*) You'll be coming with us on the ship?

      Boy smiles at Lucy.

      *Suddenly we hear a noise in the distance: Nas
      yelling, Theo shouting, his voice full of panic and
      the low moan of zombies.*

THEO Help! HELP!

      *Boy runs into the darkness in the direction of
      Theo's shouts, Lucy follows.*

*Lights up as Boy and Lucy emerge from the
darkness of the sewer into a street lit by streetlights.*

*Nas kicks and punches at the zombies
surrounding her. She's loses her bat, and Theo
watches on, with the bat at his feet. He doesn't
see Boy and Lucy behind him.*

NAS (*yelling*) Get off me! Get off me, you zombie   170
creeps!

THEO (*moaning to himself*) Oh no, why is this
happening? What am I going to do? I can't do
it, I can't do it. I have to … hang on, Nas! I'm
coming for you!   175

*Theo picks up the bat and wades into the
zombies, lashing out right and left. His eyes are
closed, but he gets in a couple of lucky shots that
take out two zombies.*

*Boy arrives, and stands beside Theo, dealing
quickly with the rest.*

*Soon there's a heap of zombie corpses on the
ground.*

NAS (*hugging Theo*) Whoa, my hero! I never thought
you had it in you!

THEO (*freeing himself from her*) Don't get used to it. That
was the scariest thing I've ever done in my life.

NAS But the point is that you did it!   180

THEO (*smiling, suddenly proud of himself*) I did, didn't I?

LUCY (*to Boy, quietly*) There you go. Sometimes people can surprise us, too.

> *Boy glances at Lucy then turns to Nas and Theo, his face grim.*

BOY Did either of you get bitten or scratched?

THEO (*deflated*) Trust him to spoil the mood.

LUCY He's only being practical, Theo. Let me look at you both.

NAS Lucy is right, Theo. We don't want to end up like Ben.

> *Theo shrugs, then Lucy carefully inspects them both for any wounds.*

LUCY (*to Boy*) They're both fine.

BOY (*nodding*) Good. (*to Nas and Theo*) What happened?

NAS We found an exit and decided to come up for a look round.

THEO And for some fresh air. I badly needed some fresh air.

NAS We'd only been out a couple of minutes, then suddenly there were zombies all over us. They came out of nowhere.

> *Boy is instantly on alert. He quickly scans the area, his eyes narrowed, checking the street for any sign of more zombies.*

BOY I had a feeling this would happen …

LUCY What do you mean?

BOY The zombies are disturbed, unsettled. They know there's fresh meat in the city somewhere and they won't rest till they find it.

THEO (*groaning*) This just never ends, does it? **205**

BOY Come on, we need to get out of here.

NAS And we still need to catch up with Jake.

Boy leads them off. As they leave, more zombies shuffle onstage in pursuit.

Fade to black.

Scene 7

A street near the old harbour.

It's early morning and a bit hazy. On one side of the street there are abandoned houses and shops. On the other is the old harbour.

Boy, Nas, Theo (who now has his own baseball bat) and Lucy come in backwards, fighting a group of zombies.

BOY Don't let them get behind us.

NAS (*yelling*) Watch out, Theo! On your right!

THEO Got it, Nas … watch out on your left!

Theo, Nas and Boy are doing the fighting, protecting Lucy.

They steadily take out one zombie after another until there's a heap of corpses in front of them.

NAS (*breathless, panting*) I can't see any more of them. You OK, Theo? 5

THEO (*panting even more*) I'm fine, getting better all the time.

BOY I think we're safe for the moment. You did well, both of you.

Nas and Theo grin and fist bump each other.

Lucy is looking happy too, although they're all tired and grubby.

THEO We really did kick some zombie butt after all! Did you see the way I took out those two in the park? I was awesome.

NAS (*laughing at him*) Hey, you're not supposed to be enjoying this.

THEO Why not? I haven't had much fun lately. I hadn't realised just how stressful being a coward can be.

NAS The end of the world isn't supposed to be fun, dummy.

LUCY And this isn't the end of the world anymore. We're going to get away from here, start a new life somewhere else. Can anyone see the dinghy?

Lucy, Nas and Theo peer to the right, into the distance.

Boy looks the other way, keeping watch in case more zombies turn up.

THEO I can't see anything much. There's a lot of mist out there.

NAS Maybe the captain should have given us a time.

THEO Oh yeah, right. Like we've all got watches that tell the right time. I haven't set mine for months. What does yours say?

NAS (*peering at her watch*) Ten past four. 30

THEO (*showing Nas his*) Eleven thirty.

LUCY No sign of Jake. I wonder where he is.

NAS I hope some zombies ate him for breakfast.

THEO (*snorting*) He's too poisonous even for them.

NAS Maybe they'll choke on him. Result! 35

> *Nas and Theo laugh and fist bump each other again.*

BOY (*over his shoulder*) We can't just stand here waiting. It's too dangerous to be out in the open like this.

LUCY We should probably find somewhere to hide until the dinghy arrives. 40

BOY One of these houses will do. We can keep watch from a window. (*to Nas and Theo*) You two – check them out, but be careful.

NAS (*nodding*) You bet. Come on, Theo – let's find ourselves a house. 45

THEO Is that a proposal? I'm too young to get married.

NAS (*rolling her eyes, but smiling*) In your dreams.

> *Nas and Theo go over to look in the doors on the other side of the stage.*

67

LUCY You and Theo and Nas don't have to do all the fighting. I could help. I did karate for a couple of years.

BOY (*smiling*) Is that so? You're clearly a girl of many talents.

LUCY Very funny. (*seriously*) You are coming with us, aren't you?

BOY I don't think you're going to let me say no.

LUCY Too right. I can be very bossy.

BOY I've noticed.

Lucy smiles, then gives him a mock frown and wags her finger.

BOY But that's OK. I like bossy girls. I always do what they —

Suddenly they hear a noise, the foghorn of a ship giving three loud blasts in the distance.

Nas and Theo come running back to Boy and Lucy.

THEO (*delighted*) No need to hide now! It's them! Fantastic! I still can't see the ship, though, or a dinghy … (*turning to look at Boy, then realising the danger*) I get it. Too much noise.

BOY (*alert and ready to fight*) Way too much. That will bring every zombie in the city right here, right to this spot.

The foghorn gives three more blasts, then we hear the familiar moaning of the zombies, and the shuffling of their feet.

*Boy raises his bat and pushes Lucy behind him,
and Theo and Nas move closer together.*

*Suddenly Jake runs on from the left. He's clearly
shocked when he sees them and skids to a stop,
and they're just as surprised.*

*They all stand looking at each other for a
moment.*

JAKE (*quickly recovering his poise, trying to look
confused*) Hey, what are you guys doing here?
Didn't you read my note?

NAS (*furiously*) What note? You're a lying, cheating
sack of —   70

JAKE The note I left you, the one that said I was
going to meet the dinghy on my own so you
wouldn't have to cross the city. Then I was
going to come back with reinforcements from
the ship.   75

THEO Oh yeah? We didn't see any note. And how
come you turned on the alarms and opened all
the doors? Sam got killed because of that. You
left us to die, just so you could pretend to be
a hero.   80

JAKE (*spluttering a little*) What are you talking about?
You can't blame me if our host's security wasn't
all he said it was.

NAS (*stepping forward, bat raised*) That's it, I've heard
enough.   85

Jake cowers, but Lucy steps in Nas's way to save him.

Nas tries to get past, but Lucy is strong and pushes her back into Theo's arms.

LUCY   No, Nas! I won't let you do it!

NAS   Why not? He deserves to have his smug, ugly face smashed in!

LUCY   Look, I know you're angry. I'm angry with him too. But we've lost so many people … we can't afford to lose any more, not even the bad ones. There aren't enough of us humans left as it is.

THEO   There would have been even less if he'd had his way.

NAS   (*still angry, turning to Boy*) What do you think, Zombie Killer? Should we let him get away with it?

JAKE   (*spluttering even more now*) Why are you asking him?

NAS   Because he's in charge, you moron.

Nas shakes off Lucy and stands beside Theo, bat raised once more.

NAS   And if he gives us the word, you die, posh boy, whether Mother Theresa here likes it or not.

Theo raises his bat.

THEO   The same goes for me. (*whispering*) Nicely put, Nas.

There's a moment of silence and standoff.

Boy is in the centre of the stage again, Lucy protecting Jake on the left. Nas and Theo are on the right with their bats raised.

The sound of zombie moaning and foot shuffling is getting louder.

Boy stares at Jake.

JAKE (*weakening under Boy's gaze*) I don't know who 105 you think you are to stand in judgement of me. When I tell the captain —

BOY Will you tell him the truth?

JAKE What … what do you mean?

BOY About what you did. 110

JAKE (*giving up at last, his shoulders sagging*) OK, look, we all make mistakes, and I'm willing to admit I made a big one. I shouldn't have done what I did, but it's like Lucy says, I'm only human. And it's all worked out, hasn't it? You're alive, and so 115 am I, thank God, although let me tell you there were times last night when I really thought I wasn't going to make it. I lost the radio, dropped the map in the dark, only got here by luck. 120

Boy exchanges a look with Lucy and smiles.

BOY (*to Jake*) You can stop now. (*nods in Lucy's direction*) She says you live. That's good enough for me.

LUCY (*smiling at Boy*) Thank you.

NAS I don't believe it! You cannot be serious!

THEO He'll only pull the same kind of stunt again.

Suddenly the ship gives another three blasts on its foghorn.

It sounds closer now, and Lucy, Nas and Theo run over to peer into the mist.

LUCY I can see the ship!

NAS And there's the dinghy!

THEO Hey, over here!

Boy has turned back to Jake – there's obviously something else on his mind.

BOY You were running. How many zombies were behind you?

JAKE (*really worried, looking over his shoulder*) Hundreds, maybe thousands, an army of them. And they can't be far away now.

Right then, a large group of zombies enters.

Jake runs, but Boy wades into them, swinging his bat.

It's complete mayhem, and a couple of zombies manage to get their hands on him before Nas and Theo run over to help.

At last they manage to kill them all.

NAS (*to Boy*) That was so cool … the best ever!

THEO   Yeah, I want to be like you when I grow up.   135

LUCY   (*running over to Boy*) Right, that's it, we're
        leaving. The dinghy is almost here. We just
        have to go down the steps …

> *But Boy doesn't move. He looks down at his hand,
> then up at Lucy.*

> *Nas, Theo and Jake are looking on, suddenly
> aware something is wrong.*

BOY   I can't come with you.

LUCY   (*upset, confused*) But why? We've been over all   140
        this, you have to come with me, Abby would
        want you to.

THEO   Abby? Who's Abby?

NAS   (*hissing at him*) Just shut up, Theo.

THEO   What? What did I say now?   145

BOY   (*to Lucy*) It's not that I don't want to.

> *Boy holds out his hand and shows Lucy a scratch.*

BOY   I can't.

> *There's a shocked intake of breath from the
> others.*

LUCY   (*shaking her head*) You could have got
        that anywhere.

BOY   A zombie caught me with its teeth just now.   150
        I felt it happen.

> *Lucy reaches out to him, tears in her eyes, but Boy
> quickly backs away.*

BOY Don't touch me. None of you should touch me.

LUCY (*pleading*) You can still come with us. Please …
we can keep you in a cabin till we find someone
who has a cure! There must be a cure!

Boy smiles, shakes his head, and holds up his bat.

BOY This is the only cure, and you know it. Nice try,
though. Abby would have said the same.

*The background moaning of zombies goes up a
notch.*

Boy looks round and becomes very business-like.

BOY Nas, you're in charge now. Get her out of here.
I'll hold them as long as I can, give you time to
get down to the dinghy.

NAS (*in tears, but holding it together*) You got it. Come
on, Lucy.

*Nas takes Lucy's arm and starts to lead her away.
It's a struggle, and Theo has to help.*

Jake runs without looking back.

LUCY No, no! We have to do something, we can't just
leave him … we have to help. (*being dragged
away*) Your name! What's your name?

*Lucy gives Boy a lingering look and desperately
reaches out to him once more, but Nas and Theo
finally manage to drag her off.*

Boy watches them go, then is left alone on the stage.

BOY (*whispering*) My name … my name is Josh.

A horde of zombies appears, moaning and shuffling.

Josh turns to face them, raises his bat, then charges headlong with a tremendous battle cry.

He is swallowed in their midst.

Blackout.

CURTAIN

The Dead Will Walk

True-life tales of zombie terror

By Christopher Edge

There's no need to be scared of zombies, right? We all know that the only place you'll ever meet brain-munching monsters is in the pages of a book or on a cinema screen. Well, don't be so sure. Read on if you dare to find out the truth behind the legend of the walking dead …

Who do the Voodoo?

As Tom Bradman explains in the introduction to this book, the zombie is originally a Voodoo idea. Voodoo is the name of an unusual religion that started in Haiti, an island in the Caribbean. Some say Voodoo priests can use powerful magic to communicate with the dead. They can even bring a dead person back from the grave, but with one terrible difference. The undead victim will be a 'zombie' – a mindless slave under the power of the Voodoo priest.

Some people believe that Voodoo priests use magic to raise the living dead, but others think there might be a more scientific explanation. A Canadian scientist called Wade Davis claimed that Voodoo priests use a poison called tetrodotoxin to turn a person into a zombie. This poison slows the drinker's heartbeat and breathing to the point where they appear to be dead. After the victim is buried, the Voodoo priest can then dig them up and bring them 'back from the dead'. The after-effects of the poison make the victim act like a zombie.

Poisonous puffer fish

The poison tetrodotoxin is found in the puffer fish. This spiky fish is eaten as a popular dish in Japan, but it can only be prepared by a trained chef. If you eat the poisonous part of the fish you will:

- Feel dizzy
- Vomit uncontrollably
- Become paralysed
- Slip into a coma
- Die.

Make sure you avoid puffer fish the next time you get fish and chips!

Walking Corpse Syndrome

This is the name given to the peculiar condition where ordinary people believe that they are actually dead. This condition is a type of mental disorder. Its cause is unknown, although some doctors believe it can be triggered by an injury to the head. In extreme cases, sufferers believe that their flesh is rotting, even though no one else can see it.

Walking Corpse Syndrome is a very rare condition, but here are some patient case files that help explain its effects:

- **Case file #1**: A 53-year-old woman in the Philippines shocked her family by telling them she wanted to be taken to the morgue to be with other dead people. The woman believed that she was already dead and kept complaining that she smelled of rotting flesh!

- **Case file #2**: A homeless man was discovered suffering from an extreme form of Walking Corpse Syndrome. As well as believing he was dead, this patient claimed that his flesh was decomposing, his insides were melting, and his brain had rotted away!

- **Case file #3**: A Scottish man who suffered a brain injury in a motorcycle crash was thought by doctors to have made a complete recovery. When he was discharged from hospital, the man was taken on holiday to a hot country to recuperate. However, the man was actually suffering from Walking Corpse Syndrome and instead of being on holiday, thought that he had been sent to Hell!

Walking Corpse Syndrome is a condition that doctors don't know how to cure. Different treatments have been tried including giving the patient's brain electric shocks (Electroconvulsive Therapy). Many sufferers eventually recover, but often lose their memory and can't explain why they believed that they were dead.

Back from the dead

Can you imagine what it would be like to wake up in a coffin with the lid sealed shut? How about waking from a coma inside a mortuary fridge? As these two medical mishaps reveal, you don't need to be a zombie to come back from the dead:

- **Case file #1**: An eighty-year-old South African man fell unconscious after suffering an asthma attack. When his family found him, they couldn't find the man's heartbeat and thought that he was dead. Instead of calling an ambulance, they called an undertaker who took the man's body straight to a morgue. Twenty-four hours later the man woke up inside a locked fridge unit used to store dead bodies. When he started to scream for help, the people working in the morgue thought he was a ghost! Eventually, the fridge unit was unlocked and the man taken to hospital where he made a full recovery from his ordeal.

- **Case file #2**: In 1996, a British woman named Daphne Banks was pronounced dead at her home by a local doctor. Placed on a stretcher and covered in a sheet, Mrs Banks was taken by an undertaker to a nearby hospital in Cambridgeshire. However, when the undertaker was helping a hospital worker put Mrs Banks's body into a morgue refrigerator they heard her begin to snore! Mrs Banks was quickly resuscitated and taken to a hospital ward to recover from her brush with death.

Could you survive a zombie apocalypse?

If the worst happens and the living dead do start to rise from their graves, do you think you could survive? Get ready by preparing a zombie survival kit. You will need:

- **Food and water supplies:** With zombies rampaging everywhere there won't be any fresh food in the shops or milk for your cup of coffee. Stock up on tinned food and bottled water that you'll be able to carry in a backpack.

- **Mountain bike:** This mode of transport will help you make a speedy escape. On a mountain bike you'll be able to outpace even the fastest zombie.

- **Motorcycle helmet:** We all know that zombies like to eat brains, so take action to keep yours safe. Wear a motorcycle helmet to protect your head

- **Weapon:** If you need to fight back against a surprise attack, use a cricket or baseball bat. One good swing should help you keep any brain-munching zombies at bay.

We would like to thank the following schools and students for all their help in developing and trialling *Already Dead*:

Biggar High School

Claire Brewster

Sean Bulloch

Ryan Evetts

Claire Fordyce

Malcolm Gordon

Scott Green

Andrew Hodge

Emma Hutchison

Emma Inglis

Douglas Keating

Asha Malik

Douglas McTaggart

Amy Millar

Emily Quincey

Terri Ramsay

James Thomson

Craig Watson

Casa Yuen